PAT GRAYBEAL

JUSTICE

and

LUCK

A MEMOIR

Published by Second Thought LLC
940 Trombley Road
Grosse Pointe Park, MI 48230

Designed by Thomas Osborne

Printed in the United States of America

ISBN: 978-0-692-92902-5

To my beloved wife, Jill,
and to our daughters, Sally and Nancy
(and a special thanks to editor
Alex Cruden for his work and patience with me)

CONTENTS

FOREWORD

Little did I know when a handsome young man entered my music education class at the University of Richmond that my life would change forever following that day. The young man's name was John Patrick Graybeal and I soon found out that he was a music major, as was I. So, many of our classes were together.

As we became better acquainted I realized the meaning of "a true Southern gentleman," for Pat (as everyone called him) was always courteous and polite as well as thoughtful, kind and helpful. He was a good listener and a problem-solver, and always had an even temper.

Later, these traits blended well with his life as an attorney, prosecutor and judge. He was able to listen to arguments by both parties during court hearings, reflect on the presentations and render an appropriate decision.

Best of all, his great sense of humor and ability to tell a story were firmly imbedded in his personality. His ability to reflect on problems and find solutions was evident throughout his life as a father and husband as well as in his professional career.

During our 64 years of married life we have experienced our share of wonderful memories along with painful and trying times, including the loss of a daughter and the attempted murder of my husband.

But this is his story to tell. I will only add that through it all Pat has been a positive force in our lives, a strength to others – friends and strangers – and a living example of Christian faith and personal strength that helped him overcome a near-death experience and return to an active life full of love, joy and happiness – and more jokes!

– JILL GRAYBEAL

CHAPTER 1

AN INTRODUCTION

All lives are special. In doing this book, I don't want to make too much or too little of mine. So it's not a long book. It includes what could be most interesting, useful, amusing or of lasting value that came to mind over several months as I reviewed my time on this earth so far.

In many ways my life has been no more extraordinary than yours. Though I've been in the news a few times, mostly I've just gone along trying to do the right thing and have some fun as well. I think of myself as one of the luckiest men alive.

———————

Some years ago, at the suggestion of my wife, I began writing a memoir, but gave it up. This time we hired an editor for me to talk to. He seems to know what he's doing. At least, most of the time he gets my sense of humor. Basically, this book is what I've told him plus what he dug up, including from family members and friends.

Just so you know what we're up to here.

CHAPTER 2

CHILDHOOD

I grew up in a family where you did what you were supposed to. Even before I understood the meaning of high expectations, my parents were always clear about what was acceptable and desirable behavior.

I can't think of enough superlatives to describe my parents.

Also, being the youngest of six children, I had plenty of other role models in the house. I had the particular advantage of seeing how my four older brothers dealt with various situations, and learning from their experiences just what a boy should do. And, for comparison, I learned from my sister as well.

Did I have any advantages as the baby of the family? If you asked the others, they'd say I was spoiled. But I thought it was just normal. Oh, when we kids had to line up for something, like on the stairs before opening Christmas gifts, I did get to be first.

Of course, we were not model children every moment of the day. But we did do things together. One vivid memory involves a day when I was around five years old. Our parents had gone out and my second brother had a bright idea: "Let's go up on the roof and see what the view is."

Ours was a two-story brick house that had an attic, and it was through there that we found our way to the top. There was quite a view, all right, including the distance from us to the ground.

It was while we were up there that our parents came home. They caught sight of us. My mother stood there for a moment and then declared: "I'm going to go in the house and sit down, and you're going get off the roof the same way you got up there."

That was not so easy. At one point I was holding onto a window gutter trying to figure out how to get inside and my sister was yelling "Let go, let go!"

"I can't let go," I explained. But somehow we all made it back in safely, together.

My full name is John Patrick Graybeal, but for reasons that included being born on St. Patrick's Day, Pat is what I've always been called. From my earliest recognition, through college and the Navy, all during my legal career and so on, it's been Pat.

We lived in Radford, a town in the western part of Virginia that was strung out along the inside of a couple of bends of the New River. Our house was in the east end and we kids went to the elementary school there, one of three in Radford. I had the same set of eight to ten friends all the way through elementary school. Not having television, we played outdoors a lot. There was room to roam. We played marbles, and games where you pretend to be someone else. I liked pretending to be a magician. As my group got older, sometimes we would play basketball on outdoor courts.

By eighth grade, like a lot of boys, when in a schoolroom I was often eager to be doing something else. It turned out that a good use of my energy was delivering newspapers, which I continued doing on into high school. For a time, my paper route took me to 160 homes per day. That was too many to carry on a bicycle, and the town was too hilly anyway. The very first house on my route was up a steep hill.

Every Saturday was collection day. Almost all my newspaper customers paid on time and were nice folks. They appreciated my work – that I stuck to it every day. I guess this was my first large lesson about the citizenry that I would later serve.

Another thing about growing up might have influenced me, and my brothers and sister, in our career choices: At the dinner table, only one person spoke at a time, and the rest listened. (Or we didn't speak because we were too busy eating.) The consideration of each person speaking in turn is, of course, courtroom decorum, and it applies as well in the other careers my siblings chose.

As children, we absorbed the principle that you should help others, serve your community and do the best you can. I'm sure of that because, as adults, each of the six of us went into careers of helping other people, our individual communities, and our country and society. Interestingly, it turned out that each of us did this within already-established structures of principles and methods.

My oldest brother served in the Navy, and later became a minister and a professor at Yale University.

My second brother served in the Navy, then became a doctor.

My third brother served in the Navy, then became a teacher.

My fourth brother served in the Army, then became a lawyer.

My sister became a teacher.

And for me there turned out to be the Navy and then the law. Mother was always talking about each of us children amounting to something, and I'm happy to note that occurred during her lifetime.

Faith came early. During childhood, any of us had to be genuinely ill to miss a service at the Methodist Church. I've been a willing churchgoer since, usually Methodist or Presbyterian. My belief is beyond easy words. I'll say, though, that music is a suitable expression and you'd often find me in the choir.

Education was the other foundation of my childhood. My mother's father was the first president of Radford College and we lived right across the street from the school. Radford College, which later became a university, began as a college to train teachers – what was called at the time a "normal school." My father taught physics and math there. At various times my mother taught high school Latin and English. And, of course, they both taught us kids a lot.

I had my own teaching experience early on, as a teenager. This came about through helping my father, who during the summers also taught driver's education. This was at a time in Virginia when you could obtain a license to drive at age 15. Which, of course, I did. And so it turned out that a cousin and I became driving instructors, working for my father, and with students older than us.

This was also a time when most cars had stick shifts rather than automatic transmissions. And with Radford being such a hilly town, learning to drive was a rigorous course of study. My cousin and I had quite a time – and made frequent use of the additional brake and clutch pedals in the cars provided for the instructors. As it happens, more than a few of our students were themselves teachers in training, mostly women. This all made for some lively summer experiences.

CHAPTER 3

MUSIC AND COLLEGE

My mother played the piano in our home and my father played saxo-phone and violin. All of us kids took up instruments. It was a family thing to do. We made our own entertainment. My four older broth-ers played (1) violin and clarinet, (2) trombone, (3) trumpet and (4) trombone and tuba. Sometimes they also sang as a quartet. And my sister played violin and piano. What we played together was mostly from the Methodist hymnbook. We didn't play pop music.

At first I was a little too young to join in. But later I took piano les-sons, like all the kids did. For a while I played the drums until some-body said "Knock it off." So I started on the tuba, because we already had one at home, and kept with it. Years later someone asked why I chose the tuba and I said "fewer notes." But seriously, I liked it. And when I got older, that's what I played in the high school band in Rad-ford.

When I was a senior, a new music teacher from Kentucky was hired by our high school. When we met, he said, "I understand you play the tuba?"

"That's right."

"I hear you're good at it."

"I suppose."

"I can get you a scholarship to go to Morehead College," he said. "I know the band director."

"Where is it?"

"It's in Kentucky. They need a tuba player."

So I went. Another stroke of luck. This was in the fall of 1949. I enrolled as a freshman and I would major in music. And it turned out that the people there were really nice, and the band was phenomenal. A lot of the musicians had been in military bands during the time around World War II and they could really knock it cold. We played march music, parade songs, classics and other pieces.

I enjoyed it there in Morehead, but it was a pretty long way from home. You might not think so today, but it was across the Smoky Mountains and a lot of other hills, and there weren't any interstate highways. There was not even a direct route between there and Radford. There was a lot that I missed about my home territory.

But my life has been a series of fortunate incidents.

After freshman year I kept up my studies by taking summer classes at Radford College. This was easy to do because, as I mentioned, our house was right across the street from the college, and Radford didn't cost much. It made economic sense to try to complete college in three years.

One day that summer a neighbor suggested I think about transferring to the University of Richmond in Virginia. She was a music student there and said it was a fine school. Now I had been to Richmond before, because my uncle lived near it, in Ashland, and taught at a nearby college. I knew Richmond was an exciting city.

I got in for that fall and things worked out well. My first day in the music room, while I was sitting there a girl walked in and I said to myself, "Oh, my gosh, am I really happy that I transferred to Richmond!" It turned out she was a music major too, a piano player. Her name was Jill Lobach.

She was from Akron, Ohio, where her piano teacher had recommended she attend the University of Richmond. Later I learned that Jill's mother was a music lover as well. For example, every Saturday afternoon they would listen to the opera on the radio while doing the ironing.

In college, in addition to music, I had a liberal arts curriculum – classes such as biology, English literature, French language and so on. I was very pleased with the professors and classes. Although brought up a Methodist, I found the Baptist program at the university was quite welcoming and supportive for students.

The music classes covered a lot of aspects. We learned about methods of music instruction and the history of music as well as details and techniques of the instruments themselves. There were not a lot of music majors, and Jill and I had a number of classes together. I was dating someone else and so was she, but as time passed, Jill and I found ourselves getting along very well together.

We began dating in the last part of senior year. We still had curfew then, though. Our solution, which fit in with our school mission, was to usher for music performances at the Mosque Theater in Richmond, which early on became known as one of the ten greatest theaters in the United States. (It's since been renovated and is now known as the Altria.) This duty gave us a fine explanation for staying out late.

At the end of the school term, when I had to perform my required vocal recital, Jill accompanied me on piano. That showed some true devotion.

9

CHAPTER 4

IN THE NAVY — AND OUR WEDDING

About six months before my graduation at the University of Richmond, I thought I should get interested in officer candidate school (OCS) for my military service. All my brothers had enlisted in the military, and my oldest brother was an officer. The OCS accepts college graduates and trains them to go into the military as first-level officers.

I went to Washington and took the OCS test. After an anxious period, news came that I passed, even though it appeared my test score was lower than what a classmate scored, and he didn't get in. Then I had to go for a full medical exam. We came to the part where a doctor examined my teeth. He frowned and said, "You've had a lot of work done, haven't you."

It was true that during childhood my teeth weren't the best and the dentist was in there a lot.

An officer happened to come in and the doctor, motioning toward me, said, "We can't take this man. He's had too much dental work."

The officer snapped back: "Take him. We want him to shoot the enemy, not bite 'em!"

So I was lucky again – into OCS at 20 years old, and I went to the Navy school in Newport, Rhode Island, for four months. This was a big step and a great break for me. The OCS purpose was to educate us in the workings of ships and naval stations, so that when we received and/or gave orders as officers we would know what we were talking about. So we took classes in such subjects as gunnery, engineering and navigation. We had daily quizzes and some excellent instructors. This was serious business – and we marched between our classrooms and dining and residence areas. We lived four to a suite and I met young college graduates from all over the country.

After graduation they were giving out the orders to each new officer. When it was my turn a chief petty officer said, "You're going to California."

I had thought I would be assigned to the big Navy complex at Norfolk. In fact I had felt so sure about it that Jill had begun a teaching job there. I said something about California not being my preference.

The chief petty officer responded: "You ever been there?"

"No."

"You'll love it."

It turned out he had a point. My assignment was to attend a communications officers short course in Monterey, a beautiful location on the Pacific coast. My group was billeted in the former Hotel del Monte, which was once known as the most elegant seaside resort in the world, and which was the forerunner of the Pebble Beach Company. We lived there and dined there, with all the ice cream you could eat. On our free time we could visit Carmel, a really good-looking town. I got to watch big golf tournaments at Cypress Point and Pebble Beach, and saw top celebrities along with the famous golfers. One day I was standing next to Hoagy Carmichael when the "Tarzan" star Johnny Weissmuller walked by.

After succeeding in this Navy postgraduate course, I received new orders. A chief petty officer told me: "You're going to San Diego."

I said something about San Diego not being my preference.

"You ever been there?"

"No."

"You'll love it."

When thinking back about my military experience, I feel so fortunate about being able to serve as a Navy officer during a time of relative peace, about the specific assignments and stations, and about all the experiences, one after another, that turned out favorably. San Diego, for example, was quite congenial and with fine weather.

As an ensign I was assigned to ship number LST-846, handling communications operations. An LST (landing ship, tank) is designed to carry vehicles, cargo and troops and unload them directly onto shorelines.

LST-846 was built in 1944 and had been re-commissioned in 1950. It was 328 feet long, with a beam (width) of 50 feet, so it was a fairly large ship – but certainly not fancy. It was operated by a dozen or so officers and about a hundred enlisted men. It could transport more than 1,800 tons.

During my time in San Diego, I received my first promotion, to lieutenant (junior grade).

Our ship was part of operations up and down the coast. Readiness exercises. We carried troops and military vehicles to designated shoreline areas for landings. Sometimes we dropped the troops off into shallow water near the shore and sometimes we ran our bow right onto the beach so the tanks and other vehicles could drive off.

After I'd been on it for a while, the 846 was sent north for repairs in Vallejo, just north of San Francisco. The work was going to take about four months. I planned to get a leave and go to Akron to get married.

We had wanted to get married sooner, but her parents didn't go along with that – and neither did mine – and at that time in Ohio if you weren't 21 yet you needed parental approval. So we had to wait. My parents thought I was too young and had the Navy commitment to carry out.

I learned that Jill's father, an insurance executive, was concerned about the economic prospects of a son-in-law who was a sailor and music major. And her mother was even more opposed, it turned out. I learned later that she thought I was "just a country boy from Virginia."

It was awkward. Jill had already bought her wedding dress and made other preparations before she knew of the parental reluctance. But I also learned that Katie, Jill's older sister, was on her side.

At this point, Jill was in Ohio and I was in California, we hadn't seen each other in months and were trying to work things out by long-distance telephone.

There were lots of arrangements to be done and problems to be solved. But finally we turned 21 and a Navy leave gave us time. I got a flight to the Akron-Canton airport. Unfortunately, Jill was waiting for me at the Cleveland airport, and when I didn't get off the plane there she went home crying and saying I wasn't coming.

But things still worked out. The church wedding on July 18, 1953, was lovely. Katie was Jill's maid of honor and the best man was my brother Charlton. Of course we had music – one of Jill's friends was the organist. We were very happy.

Jill adds:

"For the reception, Mother had planned a sit-down dinner to

which we were not invited. But we did need to make an appearance and then be on our way. Pat had worn his white Navy dress uniform for the wedding ceremony and now had to change everything to his khakis, down to his darker socks and shoes, plus his cap cover, which is a tedious process to change. It seemed to take a long time and Mother was not patient.

"But we exited and drove to Cleveland for an overnight hotel stay. Just as we arrived the entire Cleveland Indians baseball team was in the lobby and using the elevators. … That was the start of our honeymoon, which lasted four days as we drove across the country to California, mostly on Route 66. This was before the interstates. There was no decent place to eat or to stay."

Years later, Jill's sister Katie, recalling their parents' initial skepticism, said with a smile:

"But you know, Pat turned out to be quite a fine young man."

And as the years passed it became brightly clear "what an extremely well-suited couple they are."

———

When we returned to California I did my part in finishing the work on the 846. The ship then sailed back to home port in San Diego and took part in more readiness operations. Meanwhile, Jill drove to San Diego. We rented a furnished apartment and I enjoyed being there when the ship was in port. Jill had time to do things such as play golf in that wonderful weather there. I told her she had to be careful, as a junior officer's wife, not to beat any admirals on the golf course.

When ashore I could attend church, usually Methodist services and sometimes Presbyterian. Jill and I were especially interested in the churches' music programs and choirs. We lived just a few blocks from Balboa Park, which had many attractions, and we could do whale-watching while on shore. One Christmas Day we had a picnic at the beach; back home it was snowing. We did the kind of sightseeing you'd expect that people from the East would do and took trips all around. Near the end of our time in San Diego, when the first Disneyland opened, we visited. Back then you could drive right up to the gate.

At one point during my duty in the port of San Diego, I arranged that Jill could join the officers (including me) for dinner one night on the ship. I thought she would enjoy that and she seemed excited about the prospect. It would be a first for her. She would take a cab to the waterfront and then a water taxi out to the LST.

I was right on deck watching for her that evening. And there she was. Her little boat pulled up alongside the ladder that stretched from the water straight up to the deck. She looked beautiful, with a real nice skirt and high heels.

She paused, looking at the ladder, which was about thirty feet high. She glanced around and looked up at me with a question on her face. I understood. Quickly I climbed down into her boat, helped her onto the ladder and followed her up as close behind as decently possible. We got a good laugh in talking about what we hadn't thought of before planning this onboard dinner.

It was in San Diego that I played the tuba for the last time. As it happened, I got to sit in for some rehearsals with the symphony orchestra there – just in case, I guess. They found an instrument I could use. I'm not sure I was good enough for such a group, but I met some very nice people, did play in one concert and found the whole experience enjoyable.

CHAPTER 5

OVERSEAS

LST-846 received orders to sail to Japan in January 1954. So in the middle of winter Jill drove back across the country to Ohio by herself – she didn't tell her parents she was doing that because she didn't want them to worry – and arrived in Akron as a nice surprise for them.

We put out to sea. It was not a brief trip. From San Diego to the Yokosuka Naval Base near Tokyo is more than 5,600 miles. The ship's top speed was about 15 miles per hour. Our captain said that what LST really stands for is Large Slow Target, but fortunately our journey was peaceful.

During some of the time we were alone in the sea, far from points where radar would help us navigate. It turned out that part of my job was to determine our location and course by using only the stars. Celestial navigation. Another interesting experience for just a country boy from Virginia. Alone on the dark ocean and steering by starlight.

Our duties in Asia included landing operations – readiness exercises – in Iwo Jima and Okinawa. We would carry Marines and their vehicles to the islands for landings, letting them off near or on the shore, and then pick them up a few days later.

One time off Okinawa our ship was leading several others in a war games exercise at night. We were running dark – no lights at all and as silent as we could. I was on the bridge. We had one radar man scanning off the bow.

"There's something there," he told me.

"What is it?"

"I don't know," he said.

"Where is it? Are we close?"

"I'm not sure," he said.

We couldn't turn a spotlight on. So I said, "Point your antenna at where you think it is."

He did, and I changed our course slightly. The other ships followed. We never did find out what the radar man picked up, but we didn't hit it, either.

Another time, in a similar war games situation, there were some even tenser moments. On this night we were moving along the coast, also running dark and with radio silence. Strict orders. Ours was the second ship in a line of four.

Again, I was on the bridge. Suddenly our instruments detected movement in a river that emptied into the sea just ahead of us. It was a ship of some size coming down the river at a right angle to us and aimed directly at our ship's course.

Now we could glimpse its lights. By every indication, its pilot had no idea we were in his path.

The commanding officer was in his quarters below. I ordered a sailor to go ask him whether we should show our lights – in violation of our mission – or chance a collision.

The moments ticked by. I watched the radar blip, blip, blip, confirming that the unaware coastal craft was closing in on us and could strike the side of our ship.

The sailor returned.

"What did he say?" I asked.

"He didn't respond, sir."

A number of thoughts flashed through me. Where they intersected was at one conclusion: I was going to have to make the decision.

Now.

I thought of a court-martial.

I thought of a collision.

We turned on all our running lights.

The oncoming ship – smaller and more maneuverable than ours – swerved away, obviously startled.

No collision.

And I've yet to be summoned for breaking orders. I think it's been mentioned that I have been lucky.

For a while I also served on LST-1123, nearly identical to the 846, and our stops included the Korean coast – and without incident, fortunately.

A couple of other things occurred while I was in Asia that make for interesting stories – interesting as long as you were not the chief participant. As it happens, a dental situation was involved in each.

One episode took place while I was on shore patrol duty at the Yokosuka base. The last-call boat – the final one of the evening that left from shore and made the rounds of the various Navy ships in the harbor – shoved off at 11 p.m. One night at the last moment, a very inebriated sailor lurched aboard, slumped down and vomited. In doing so he expelled his false teeth.

That made it even harder for him to talk.

So I asked around the boat if anyone knew which ship this man was assigned to.

No clue.

I had one last hope. We fished out his teeth, and at each naval ship we came up to I held up the set and hollered, "Does anybody know if the sailor with these teeth is one of yours?"

It was a long night.

The other story of things that did not go quite right took place at an Army camp at the base of Mt. Fuji. As it happened, the camp's commanding officer, a captain, had invited a very attractive young lady to join a dinner party where I was also a guest.

She arrived early and went into conference with the captain. Then, for some reason, she took a shower. She emerged in time for the dinner, in a distinctively attractive dress. But after she sat down she did not seem comfortable. Her squirming prompted a conversation aimed at helping her relax.

Well, it transpired that after her shower she had used some powder that she thought was talcum. In fact, it was the captain's Fasteeth denture adhesive. She had glued herself to her dress.

All told, I was in the Far East for about eleven months.

I was not involved in active combat, but toward the end of my duty tour, Vietnam got hotter. We sailed to Saigon and unloaded some vehicles, then made our way north up the coast and tied up on a river next to a French Foreign Legion post. Helicopters from our ship flew support and readiness missions.

The French had been fighting in Indochina, including Vietnam, since 1946. After President Dwight Eisenhower took office in early 1953, the United States had increased aid to the French troops so they could put down the Chinese-supported Communists in the area. But the Communists kept up their efforts, and on May 7, 1954, the French made a military surrender at Dien Bien Phu, in northwest Vietnam.

On the ship, what we saw was just a very small part of the geopolitical picture. We took some pro-French Vietnamese soldiers back south to the Saigon area – and a jeep with less than 15 miles on the odometer. This vehicle had been brought from the U.S. about half a year previous for use by our ally. Talk about a low-mileage special! But, as you've just read, some odd things can happen when the military is involved.

From Saigon we sailed for Japan. We entered Tokyo Bay around dawn. As we slowly motored in, through the semi-darkness, I saw this massive form on the land, back from the shore. I gradually lifted my head, looking higher and higher. This solid form kept rising, up, up, up. Then the sun's rays hit the top of it – it was Mount Fuji! I stood there and marveled. What a glorious sight for a young man from Virginia's Blue Ridge territory.

After extending my military tour by 10 months, to coordinate my release to coincide with the fall term in graduate schools, I completed my active duty in San Diego without harm to anyone, including myself.

CHAPTER 6

SETTING THE COURSE

It was September 1956 and I was a free man and back on home ground in Virginia. Doing something productive was a necessity. My college degree was a BS in Public School Music, but at that point in my life I did not want to be a teacher. One of my brothers had become a lawyer, and while I was in the Navy both he and Jill had said: Why don't you go to law school? The way my brother talked about his experience got me particularly interested.

I looked into enrolling at the University of Virginia Law School. But the fall term had begun and they were full. Also, I learned, obtaining a degree there would take three years. That would be expensive. And there were no nearby teaching job vacancies for Jill.

So I checked with the University of Richmond, since I had a good experience there earning my bachelor's degree, and talked with the dean of the university's T. C. Williams School of Law. At the end of our conversation, he said, "I guess if you start Monday and don't miss any classes," it might work out.

And it did. Again, lucky me. I had a scholarship position in the law library, the professors were excellent, and I enjoyed my courses, particularly regarding real estate and in criminal law. There were about three dozen people in my class (three women). By also taking summer classes, I was able to graduate two years later with a law degree. While I studied, Jill taught in the Henrico County schools and in the summers worked for the county parks and recreation department.

During law school, as I thought about areas of specialization, I became certain that I did not want to be part of a very large firm or work in a big city. So I learned to be a general practice attorney who could handle criminal cases.

I talked with my lawyer brother about joining in his practice after graduation, but he was in a small town and, being the newest attorney there, was not flush with business. So I set up in Christiansburg, Virginia, which was the county seat of Montgomery County and quite close to my hometown of Radford. Christiansburg was also where my doctor brother had his practice.

CHAPTER 7

FIRST IMPRESSIONS

In 1959, Christiansburg was still a small community. Ann Carter and her family were there, and she recalls:

"A young couple moved in to the house behind ours. We could see across our backyards. My first thought was what a nice-looking, fine couple. ... He was really a handsome fellow in that Naval Reserve uniform."

As time passed, Ann, her family and the Graybeals became lifelong friends, which proved especially important later at two times of great stress.

Nancy Nixon and her husband, Sam, were new in town as well. Nancy was in her first year of being a teacher there and Sam was starting an insurance business in a one-room office upstairs from a mens-wear store.

In another one-room office next door to Sam's was a young man also new in town and just starting his law practice – J. Patrick Graybeal. "The two men were not that busy and had plenty of time to talk," Nancy recalls. Then she met Jill Graybeal, who was just starting her own teaching job. Everyone was congenial. Nancy says:

"One day Sam said why don't we all go to supper on Friday night when we're all done working for the week.

"We went to a place called the Outpost, which was a farmhouse converted to a restaurant, and we had such a good time we decided we would do that every Friday. … Pat and Sam would tell jokes and funny stories, sometimes about the ne'er-do-wells they had for clients, being new in town. We had such a good time together, always laughing.

"My first impression of Pat? Marvelous, funny, handsome … and down to earth."

The Friday nights continued until the Nixons and the Graybeals each had their first child – one a son, the other a daughter – in 1961, deepening the friendship.

Jill recalls that during the late 1950s that she and Pat, Nancy and Sam, and two other couples formed a bridge club. They weren't serious bridge players but it was a lot of fun. Then, as it happened, each of the four women became pregnant around the same time.

In 1964, the Nixons and the Graybeals each had their second child. This time both were girls – and they became friends for life as well.

CHAPTER 8

DEFENSE AND PROSECUTION

So I was the newest defense attorney in town. As is typical in such situations, I received court appointments to represent indigent defendants, almost always in criminal cases. At the time I did not know how valuable the experience would become. I knew only that these were poor people who, by law, deserved an able lawyer.

Meanwhile, Jill had resumed teaching. One way or another, throughout our life together, Jill has been a teacher. She has taught music to elementary, middle and high school students, and – because one school needed her to – special education and physical education as well. Adept at playing the organ as well as piano, she has taught choral music and led choirs, which she loved to do. She has, of course, taught me more than a thing or two.

In Montgomery County, she began teaching music in the public school system. In 1961, after we'd been there more than two years, she gave birth to our first child, Sally, and then our second, Nancy, was born in 1964.

All this time I remained in the Navy as an officer in the Reserve, where you were expected to do two weeks of active duty annually.

This usually meant a cruise (which was not at all like what tourists experience), but after several years I was able to stay ashore and use my legal abilities with the Fifth Naval District in Norfolk, Virginia. By serving in good standing in the Reserves, I was able to earn promotions – which increased my pay and pension. I retired as a lieutenant commander in 1973 after a total of twenty-one years in the Navy.

Back in Montgomery County, as a young attorney with a lot of lower-level criminal cases, I was becoming a familiar figure at the courthouse. Often I represented defendants in trials, and on the other side was a prosecutor who had been elected to that job time and again for decades. This was another learning experience and, again, one that had a fortunate outcome for me.

In late 1964 this longtime prosecutor died. A successor was needed immediately. The judge whose job it was to make the interim appointment considered who was available. The other ten or so lawyers in town who were qualified each had established practices and did not want the job. So the judge appointed the new guy. I was 32 at the time.

But, as it turned out, I did OK in the job and subsequently was elected six times to four-year terms, meaning I served until 1989. Over those years, a few other lawyers ran for the office, but they told me the only reason they were in the race was to publicize their law practices – outright advertising by lawyers was considered unethical in those days – and they did not actually want to be elected.

It was a busy position. In my last full year of doing it I prosecuted almost 700 cases at trial.

When I started the job, the office consisted of one fulltime secretary and one who worked part-time. So I handled all the cases. Later, as the population grew, both secretaries worked full hours and I was able to hire an assistant prosecutor, and sometime after that a second one to work part-time.

Mary Huff met Pat shortly after the Graybeals moved to Christiansburg. They met in a Laundromat. Later, Mary recalls:

"After our daughters became best friends, Pat called to ask me to come work for him. I was too much in awe to call him back."

But he called her again, and she agreed to a part-time job as his secretary in the office of the commonwealth's attorney, which was the official title of the county prosecutor. She remembers:

"I was never a star pupil in shorthand, but he was patient. He would dictate a letter and then he would come over and read my shorthand and tell me what it said."

They have been friends ever since.

The case load grew along with the county's population, of course, and my first decade in office coincided with a substantial expansion of the Virginia Polytechnic Institute in nearby Blacksburg, which during that time became a state university and was growing by about one thousand students each year.

In general, the students of Virginia Tech were no more criminally minded than anyone else, but this was a time of social turmoil in the United States. In particular, along with other young adults, students were being drafted to fight in Vietnam.

As a historical digest posted later by the university notes, "students became more aware of national and international issues. Recognizing the impact of these issues on their own lives, they sought more involvement in decisions affecting them," sometimes in ways that violated the law. In 1970, for instance, a student protest occupation of the university's Williams Hall led to more than one hundred arrests on trespassing charges.

A more difficult situation took place in May 1971, when several days of protests about campus student-life policies included window-breaking in downtown Blacksburg, several bomb threats (with no bombs found), detonation of a homemade tear-gas bomb in a university snack bar and a 3 a.m. fire in a campus building.

Our police tried to be non-confrontational in these circumstances. As did I. At one point I happened to be on campus and saw that another downtown protest was in the making. When a vigorous mass of students formed with some fire in their eyes, I went over asked those in the front to pause and consider a choice. You can proceed, I said, and most likely you will be arrested, or you can return to your campus life now. With it being their choice, the students turned back.

The incidents of physical damage worked against the protest cause. As the university's historical digest says: "Most of the students who had been demonstrating were shocked by the burning of Bldg. 253 and the other acts of destruction and, wanting no part of such events, stopped participating in demonstrations. The campus then returned to relative normalcy."

Normalcy was fine with me. I was getting along well with the local police chiefs and their forces, who seemed to me to be well-trained and good at their jobs.

In our county's system of criminal justice, like many across the country, accountability followed a regular path. If the police arrested you, you were taken before a magistrate for a brief hearing, at the end of which one of three things usually happened: You were released on your own recognizance to appear later in court, you posted bond (with cash and/or pledge) in order to be released for that court appearance, or you were jailed until your court date. Usually, going to jail meant you were too poor to post the bond or what you were accused of doing was so alarming the magistrate decided you needed to be detained until being tried.

It was in court that you were found guilty or not, and it was my job to present the appropriate evidence against you.

Throughout the process, from before the arrest on to the court's final decision, those of us in authority had to decide one central question: Was the alleged offense against the law or just something the neighbors didn't like?

Most of the alleged offenses either involved property – theft, larceny, breaking and entering – or driving. A significant number of others involved fighting. The cases of people arrested in connection with these offenses usually were decided in District Court, where typically I would spend two days a week presenting the reasons to find the defendants guilty. A third day was usually in Juvenile and Domestic Relations Court, and from time to time I appeared in Circuit Court, where appeals and felony cases – crimes of greater seriousness – were heard and decided.

The late 1960s and early 1970s were a time when a national concern arose by young people experimenting – or worse – with illegal drugs. I found myself pleasantly surprised that there was so little of that at Virginia Tech. The undercover agents and other police found no major problems on the campus.

One deterrent was a university rule that anyone caught would be expelled. This would be a major blow to students and families who had worked hard to gain entrance to the university. For many, higher education was not an opportunity worth risking.

In any of the cases and courts, my aim was to follow the law and present any evidence that it had been broken. It was someone else's job to write the law in the state legislature, and the judge's job – sometimes with a jury – to make the final decision. For those who were guilty, the law for each kind of offense provided a minimum and maximum sentence. I didn't think it was my role to tell a judge, or our community, exactly how long a sentence should be imposed.

In sum, carrying out my job did not involve questions of what I liked or didn't like, and the community seemed satisfied. My office received very few complaints, and every four years the voters said: Keep at it.

The job title was commonwealth's attorney because the justice system is a responsibility of the state government and the official name of our state was the Commonwealth of Virginia. So I tried to protect the common wealth of the county – the wealth of social order, accountability and reliable justice.

Other than to mention some amusing or especially interesting moments (and without naming names), I did not talk about the job very much with Jill. Nor did she with me. We were both employees of the same county government (and each of us could quite possibly be dealing with the same student), so it made sense to keep things separated. And while Jill of course knew that part of my job was sending criminals to prison, I really did not want to give her anything in the way of specifics that would cause her extra concern. I could not predict what would soon happen.

What I most enjoyed about being the prosecutor was ensuring that trials were fair, that everyone involved understood what the law was, and that people could feel secure within the justice system.

What was hardest was seeing the victims of terrible acts and only being able to bring justice after the fact.

CHAPTER 9

THE BOMBING

On Dec. 4, 1973, I worked late at the courthouse in Christiansburg. Earlier that day we had more than twenty cases in court, and I stayed on in the office to finish preparing for the next day's reporting by probationers plus the seven cases I was to prosecute in Circuit Court trials. I also stopped by an election victory party for Madison Marye, a local Democrat who had won a first term as a state senator. I didn't get home until after 11:30 p.m.

After parking my borrowed car in the driveway, with the outside lights being on I noticed something odd – a Pringles potato chip can on the top of our family car, which Jill had been using that day. I thought that perhaps Jill been grocery shopping and had forgotten this can was still outside, or that one of our daughters had left it there.

So I picked up the can. It felt a little heavy. I was about to examine it when it exploded.

I didn't know exactly what had happened.

I realized an instant or two later that I was still standing and I was against the car. My hands felt like they were frozen, extremely cold. I swung back around to put my elbows on the fender of the car and started leaning my hands together trying to touch them and I couldn't feel a thing.

Blinded, I couldn't see anything to tell what had happened to my hands or anything around me. Later I learned I'd also been burned and cut on my face, chest, abdomen and legs.

I started calling for help. Jill must have run out from inside the house. I heard her say "Oh, my God, Pat, your hands!"

The Roanoke Times reported: "In spite of his injuries, witnesses said he was conscious. … Christiansburg Police Lt. A. L. Hale said that immediately after the explosion, Graybeal told onlookers to 'find the Pringles can, and you'll know what happened.'"

People rushed to help, and a rescue squad took me to the Montgomery County Hospital in nearby Blacksburg.

The police got on the case immediately. They said there was no initial indication of who might have done it. People floated several theories about a possible motive. FBI and State Police evidence experts began analyzing what was found in and around the driveway.

Jill told the police that, about 15 minutes before I arrived home, someone called the house asking about me. He didn't say who he was. She told him that I wasn't home and she offered to take a message. He hung up.

Lt. Hale told The Roanoke Times: "We're in the dark. He could be any one of a thousand people. When you're in a law enforcement position, you make enemies every day."

While for the next several days no public announcement was made, the police did get a lead. It came from a prisoner, who said: Frank DeWease did it.

Five years previously, I had prosecuted DeWease for the beating and strangling death of his wife, Ann Mae DeWease.

The bombing occurred less than a week after Frank DeWease, 39, was paroled from a 20-year sentence.

The informant was Billy Harris, who happened to be temporarily in the Montgomery County Jail on an unrelated case. Harris told the authorities:

"I pulled time with DeWease at Bland Correctional Farm. ... I was serving time there for forgery, and DeWease was there for murder. ...

"While we were together, DeWease on more than one occasion said he would like to kill everyone having anything to do with the court in Christiansburg. He said he would like to get them all in the courthouse and blow it up. He included ... Pat Graybeal. ... He seemed to want to kill Graybeal real bad. ...

"He showed me how he planned to make the bomb. He had a can and he hooked up batteries, wire and a light bulb and showed me how the bulb lit up when the can tilted to make electrical contact. The bulb was to show that if it lit up explosives would also explode. ... He said he had a source for getting dynamite from a friend who worked in a rock quarry."

Police also interviewed a café employee who was with DeWease just before and after the bombing. The employee, Clarcie Fitzwater, said:

"Frank DeWease came in about 3 p.m. He stayed there until about 5:30 or 6 p.m. During this time, he was talking to me and trying to get me to quit my job and come to his trailer and live in and keep house for him. He said he didn't have a wife and asked me if I would rather work in a beer joint or keep house for him. I thought he was a decent guy so I quit my job and went with him."

That night, she and DeWease and a few other people drove to Christiansburg, she said, with DeWease telling them exactly where to go. He had a box with him. At a certain point, he had them stop the car and he got out, she said. He was gone about half an hour.

Then they drove back to the trailer where, she said, "Frank showed me some newspaper clippings of where he killed his wife. He told me to read them. Then he showed me this picture of his wife in the casket and told me if I ever told on him or went out on him … that I would be just like her. He told me to keep the picture to remember by.

"[Then] Frank told me about Pat Graybeal being blown up. When I read the newspaper clippings I saw where Graybeal was in his wife's case. He told me he had blown him up. He said I'm damn sure I did it."

DeWease was arrested at the trailer on Dec. 13.

Found guilty at trial, he was sentenced to 24 years in prison. He was released in 1998 and went on to commit more crimes.

The most recent news about him that I know of is a Jan. 21, 2015, arrest and jailing in Roanoke County, Virginia, on five charges of probation violation involving felonies.

At an appropriate time after the attack, I put in for workers compensation benefits, given that the injuries were a result of doing my job. The claim was rejected. The government of the county, which was self-insured, said I was not eligible under a Code of Virginia rule that required that an injury occur "in the course of the employment."

A late-night explosion in my driveway was not in that course, the state Industrial Commission also decided. Its ruling said, in part:

"A claimant must prove that his injury arose out of his employment as well as during the course of his employment before compensation can be awarded. No public servant has paid a higher price for public service than has the claimant … and our sympathies are totally with him. However, an award cannot be bottomed on sympathy and the Industrial Commission has no legal basis on which to predicate an award."

Fortunately, an appeal that reached the Supreme Court of Virginia overturned that legal reasoning.

My case later influenced a similar ruling by the Supreme Court of South Dakota, though it appears I had to die in the process. This court's unanimous 1979 decision involving workers compensation "in the course of" employment said: "Another case which we find particularly persuasive involved the death of a prosecuting attorney from Montgomery County, Virginia ... John Patrick Graybeal."

CHAPTER 10

REBUILDING

When I saw Jill at the hospital, the first thing I said was "Have I lost my hands?"

This was a really hard moment for both of us.

As she tried to answer, I realized I couldn't hear, and I could barely see her.

The hearing loss lasted for three days, during which I wasn't very good at reading lips either. I'm sure the severe burns on my face didn't make it easier for people to talk with me.

The county hospital put me in separate area where I was the only patient and Jill could stay with me. Police guarded it. The Marriott sent family dinners over.

There was really an outpouring of support from the community. It seemed like everyone helped us! One couple of our friends took our daughters in – they were then 11 and 9 – and another couple cared for our new puppy. That is friendship!

The bomb had damaged our house, including blowing out the windows. Until the house could be secured, a deputy sheriff sat in the living room with a rifle.

Soon we had a home security system, and ones were also provided for all the county judges. The bombing turned out to be the only such attack in our region during the half-century that I was involved in the criminal justice system.

After my condition improved enough, I went to a specialist in Charlottesville who did an excellent job, one ear at a time, in bringing my hearing back as much as possible. And I had a terrific surgeon who was extremely careful in removing pieces of the potato chip can from my eyes.

In brief, the permanent damage was loss of my hands and forearms, scarring in various places, diminished hearing and eye damage (tiny particles of metal are still in there).

Recovery was anything but brief, yet it had its lighter moments. I learned more of the details about the moments after the bomb went off. It's remarkable what odd things you do and say and notice at a time of extreme crisis. For instance, Jill recalled how, just after the rescue squad arrived, it looked like they were going to slice open my suit to get it off me. She yelled to them, "Please don't cut his suit. It's brand-new." It also had both of our paychecks in a jacket pocket, and we sure didn't want those sliced either.

For a time, my recovery was at home. One morning we received a beautiful surprise when the choir from the nearby Presbyterian church came to our back door at breakfast and sang Christmas carols.

Charlton, my doctor brother who lived near us, was a big help as a medical advocate and good companion. On the day after Christmas, he drove me to the Bethesda Naval Hospital just outside Washington for specialized treatment. For some reason they put me in the VIP area there, along with such people as Hubert Humphrey, the former U.S. vice president who was then a senator representing Minnesota. I saw the famous Admiral Hyman Rickover, known as the father of the nuclear Navy, walking the hospital corridors for his exercise.

We went to downtown Washington for my prostheses and I learned to use them at Bethesda over a couple of weeks. One of the surprising things was still having the sense of thumb and finger feelings.

The clamp hooks were a great help. Now I could pick up and read a book, feed myself and do a lot of the other usual things. And I could write just about as badly as I did before.

There are a couple of things I probably shouldn't tell you about my time in Bethesda. One was that the occasional beer somehow found its way into my room. However, my brother agreed that it had a certain therapeutic quality. And there was the time a nurse was doing an exceptionally thorough job of using an instrument to listen to my heartbeat. She put it on my chest, here and there, and then went on to various places on my back. For some reason, maybe connected to my musical background, I began a low steady hum, I guess just to give her something more to listen to. I still remember that feeling of the really cold cream she slapped on my back.

The Bethesda hospital people were very good to me. They gave me the foundation for my life to proceed unhindered.

My daughter Sally's best friend at this time and for a number of years was Shannon Huff, my secretary Mary's daughter. She's Shannon Huff Sherman now, and she told my editor:

"In our small town, the attack on Pat at his home was terribly shocking to us as children. We were introduced to evil."

But, Shannon recalled, the Graybeals stayed just as strong as ever. Even though the situation was so difficult for them, they went on with their lives, and by their example and their faith they made us feel safe. They showed us a life lesson in how to deal with a very difficult situation.

"Pat never lost his cool. He was always a very together person."

Shannon remembered being with Sally when her father was at Bethesda Naval Hospital and she got a letter from him, handwritten with his prosthetic hooks. That was an amazing moment, she said.

I've been asked how the bombing affected my religious faith, and my answer is: The experience affirmed it. I regained sight, hearing, the ability to work. My life could go on. Jill and our daughters were unharmed. My faith was strengthened.

All along, my legs were not badly affected by the bomb and I could walk around as needed, but it was clear to me that I wouldn't be of much use if I couldn't drive. So I rigged up a cord arrangement on the steering wheel and started taking short, careful trips. The courthouse was only about a mile from home and I was determined to work a full schedule with my own transportation. Or at least try. You don't know what you can do until you are there. Each one of us has to decide, but it seems to me that self-pity serves no purpose.

Apparently nobody in our town had ever seen a double amputee like me, but most people were supportive. Many people that we knew casually seemed to feel an awkwardness when I worked at doing normal things with my clamp hooks and prosthesis forearms. Of course, with no experience in these matters, they weren't sure how to help me, or how much, and they usually didn't ask what they wanted to know. Much more often it would be a complete stranger who would ask the most direct questions. And children. I was happy to explain how it worked to children, but their parents were always quick to interrupt in the name of politeness.

I was out of work for four months. In my first case back in front of a jury, I was kind of shaky at first. It wasn't anything about the case or the facts; it was just hard to keep from breaking down. But I knew I had to keep going. What happened to me was just one incident caused by one person among thousands I had dealt with. That's what I knew and that's how I could get back to doing the job.

CHAPTER 11

COPING AND HELPING

Pat's secretary Mary Huff recalls:

"I worked for him before and after the bombing. ... The time right after the bombing, those were dark days, no sunshine, a lot of sadness. ... But he was never bitter, never complained. Even after that awful decision when the county said he would not receive workers' compensation. ..."

Right after the bombing, she would go with Jill to the hospital, where Pat was in the separate and secure wing. "The walls were covered with flowers, they were everywhere. I helped Jill with the thank-you notes."

When Pat returned to work, in the beginning there were moments of awkwardness. Pat would go around as if everything were normal, including pulling the big law books off the shelves in order to look things up.

"I wasn't sure what to do," Mary said. "I didn't know when to offer or what to offer. ... But he just made it easier for all of us. He came back with a determination and he came back upbeat. ... He had a remarkable sense of humor and it got all of us through."

Pat began taking a legal secretary to court with him. Soon all the other attorneys did, too. "It was a good thing. ..."

Pat just got right back to work with the same full attention to his job, Mary remembered. But there was one moment during a trial that gave him pause. "There was one case where a woman was accused of assaulting her husband by hitting him on the head with a frying pan. When Pat asked her why she hit her husband, she said, 'I got the pan because I just up and wanted to fry me up a steak.' Pat couldn't help but think about that for a while."

After she went on to another job, Mary remained close friends with the Graybeals. For three years she and Jill both worked for the school district. Mary recalled how, at church, Pat sang in the choir and Jill was the choir director. "I used to tell Pat a lot that he had a voice made for radio and television, and he'd just shrug it off."

Backyard neighbor and friend Ann Carter also recalls that after the attack, Pat showed no bitterness at all. "He was content within his own self. ... It was just amazing to me, the inner peace he had. ... He would have been a fine minister."

Shannon Huff Sherman remembers watching Pat in action in court a few times after he had been attacked. She said he always showed compassion and respect to people on all sides. Some years later she met a man who had been a teenage defendant in the Montgomery County court system. When he learned that she knew Pat Graybeal, he said he had strong memories of how Pat was so kind and fair to him even though he'd caused trouble.

Ann Carter remembers the time before Pat went on his first out-of-town business trip after the attack. Jill was very upset that she would be unable to go with him. How was he going to be able to manage? But Pat always accepted help from others, showing no resentment about his situation, Ann confirms.

Nancy Nixon, the friend whose first impression of Pat was that he was marvelous, funny, handsome and down-to-earth, remembers that he remained that way despite the attack. Her recollection:

"I didn't know about the bombing until the next morning." She learned where the family was and rushed to see them, asking if there was anything at all she could do. "They were just grey with worry," she recalls, but Jill did mention their dog Freddie, a puppy they had recently acquired and which was temporarily housed with a veterinarian.

When Nancy insisted she would take care of the dog, Pat's smiling response was "Oh, Freddie the Freeloader."

Later, when Pat returned to Christiansburg from Bethesda with his prostheses, Nancy recalls that, one day, she was at a teller's window at the bank and Pat was at the window next to hers. "I'm always curious," she said, including about "his hooks," so she watched in subdued amazement how Pat nonchalantly and deftly took out his deposit slip and conducted his transaction just like anyone else in the bank that day.

"He's such a sweet man," Nancy said. "They are treasured friends."

CHAPTER 12

BACK ON THE JOB

Just about every day, I saw, some people came to the courthouse without fully realizing what they had got themselves into. These were people charged with their first criminal offense. Often, at the time they were arrested, they were belligerent, upset, angry or worse. By the time they appeared in court as defendants, in general they were calmer and more receptive. As prosecutor, usually my first choice with such first offenders was to recommend probation if they pleaded guilty.

Most of the time probation worked. Being ordered to stay clean in order to stay free gave people the chance to avoid the kinds of things that had gotten them arrested – certain companions, too much alcohol, the unchecked impulse toward larceny. Most of these first offenders were caught stealing or fighting or driving drunk, and the experience of being processed to face possible imprisonment became a memorable event.

I had found it helpful to occasionally ride with sheriff's deputies at night, to get a first-hand view of what they faced, how they handled it and what happened during arrests. One such instance turned out to be particularly memorable. At this time there had been a series of arsons, including some on church grounds.

When two deputies and I drove by one church that night and saw a single car almost hidden around back, we quickly pulled in.

Well, it turned out that the couple in the car were producing some heat, but they clearly had no interest in setting the church on fire.

Three weeks later, at a wedding reception, I walked over to where a woman was pouring from the punchbowl, and we recognized each other from that night behind the church. Her faced turned red. Without a word, I looked for a drink elsewhere in the room.

An incident on another night involving a couple was full of tension, but some laughter as well. The deputies' car that I was in received a radio call about trouble at a house up on the river, possibly a serious domestic dispute.

At the house, the deputies announced their arrival and went on in. They found a woman trapped against the wall – by a waterbed. This was at a time when waterbeds had just become a big fad, and the couple in this house apparently had been putting theirs to vigorous use. One side of the frame had broken off, and the bag of water was pinning the woman down.

The guy was panicked about saving his girl. He pointed at the bag and yelled "Shoot it! Shoot it!"

"We don't shoot water mattresses," the lead deputy explained, aiming for calm.

After the woman was freed without injury, we had a good laugh back in the car, and for some time afterward.

Most law enforcement situations were more serious, of course, and whatever humor was involved tended toward the macabre. One such situation came when police in the city of Radford as well as the county sheriff's department were notified that a body had been discovered. I was with the deputies who responded. The corpse was by the side of the road, leaning against a city limits sign. A Radford officer was there, too, and declared: "It's your case, boys. He's leaning on the county side of the sign."

Montgomery County was not heavily populated, and this was a factor when a trial needed a jury. On occasion it could take a long time to put together twelve eligible people and have none of them know any of the people involved in the case.

My approach to jury selection was to play it straight. Otherwise you can out-guess yourself, with unfortunate consequences. I recall one case where the defense attorney insisted on a jury trial and then approved the set of jurors. His client was readily convicted and sentenced to jail. Other lawyers familiar with the case said that if the trial had been put in the judge's hands instead of a jury's, the outcome would have been probation.

The play-it-straight method worked best for me during a trial as well. My strategy was simply to make clear how the law fit the facts of the case.

The majority of cases didn't go to trial but instead were settled with plea agreements. The lawyers on both sides generally knew each other and valued consistency and trust. A "gotcha" technique just wouldn't play well when you know you'll be back in court many times in the future with the same players.

One place I'd see a few of those players was at the lunch counter at the Thompson-Hagan drugstore (which is still in business), one of the few places to get a lunch in what was still a small downtown.

In general, the people in local government, including law enforcement, got along well enough. In particular, I was never made to feel any pressure about going easy on someone with connections or influence. I can't recall any such circumstance. And I'd like to think that anybody who knew me wouldn't have tried.

I was careful, too. Two dozen years as prosecutor without so much as a traffic ticket.

Someone asked me what my daughters thought about me in my work. When they were old enough to understand, what impressed them the most was that their friends knew I was the man who gave out the driver's licenses to first-time drivers. I always gave them a talk, too. My daughters reported that it was a good one.

We had busy lives in those years. In addition to being parents and both Jill and I having fulltime jobs, in a typical week there'd be a Rotary meeting on Monday, a school board meeting on Tuesday, choir practice (me singing and Jill directing) on Wednesday, a Naval Reserve meeting on Thursday in Roanoke and activities involving the children and friends on various days.

For many years I was a director of the Cambria Bank/First Virginia Bank of the Southwest, and I served on quite a few committees and associations connected with the judicial system. With the Rotary I was a Paul Harris scholar and also for a time was the president of the Christiansburg-Blacksburg Rotary. I'd been president of the Radford-Montgomery unit of the American Cancer Society. Representing the National College of District Attorneys, I was a presenter on the subject of trial tactics at conferences in Philadelphia, New Orleans, Puerto Rico and North Carolina. I spoke at high school graduations and other community events and many meetings of civic organizations.

Well, they asked me to.

CHAPTER 13

SALLY AND DAD

Our daughters Sally and Nancy grew up during the time that I was prosecutor.

Let's talk about Sally, because she's no longer here to talk for herself. Sally was dynamite – in a good way. She got things going. She was really creative. And she was always about three steps ahead of me in thinking about things to do for others.

After college, Sally succeeded as a graphics designer, working for museums and universities. She created her own business, a design company that she later sold. She was part of a gourd orchestra in Richmond.

And she was a garden fairy. Seriously. She did this for the Lewis Ginter Botanical Garden in Richmond, one of the finest such gardens in the country. As garden fairy she wore a very elaborate costume and guided people around, including children of course, and thoroughly brightened everyone's day.

Shannon Huff Sherman remembers how her friendship with Sally grew:

"I met Sally in elementary school and by seventh grade we were great friends." The first time she got to know Sally's father was when the girls played at Sally's house. "Our antics amused him," she recalls.

"I was a little in awe" because of his position in the town as prosecutor but "I saw right away that he was kind, a good, good person," very intelligent and warm. "I always felt welcome in their home."

One time, when the girls were in seventh grade, their slumber party group got tickets to see a concert by Three Dog Night, a rock group that was really popular among young people. Pat volunteered to drive them all – it was a long way – and he sat through the whole show with them. "He was really a good sport."

Shannon recalls that Sally and Pat were extremely close, with similar personalities and sense of humor. Sally grew to be "a very dear person, kind and caring, like her parents. She was extremely smart and conscientious ... and beautiful. ... Everyone liked her. ...

"She was so much fun to be with," even later when she was doing chemo for her breast cancer. "We had some of the best times during the worst times," Shannon said.

Sally Graybeal died of breast cancer in 2007, at age 46.

Chris Minnigh met Pat and Jill Graybeal in 1988, soon after he began dating their daughter Sally, and after marrying her he got to know the Graybeals well over the years. After Sally's death, the Graybeals continued to treat him as a family member.

Chris recalls his first impressions and what followed:

"I met Sally at a gym in the Richmond area. I was on a stationary bike, going all out like always. She got on the next bike, which was the only open one. We started talking. I'd gone to Virginia Tech, which is right next to her hometown. We saw each other again at the gym, and then we started dating. ..."

By the time Sally took Chris to meet the family, he had learned her father was the commonwealth's attorney for the county, "and my first worry was whether I'd done anything wrong in college. But he didn't come across like a prosecutor. The first thing I noticed was his sense of humor. He likes to laugh. He likes to make you feel comfortable. ... I never saw him show any stress from his work. ...

"Everyone in the family seemed genuinely humble, empathetic, always thinking about the other person. ...

"Sally's parents lived up to every possible dream I could have about in-laws." Just being in the same room with the Graybeals "made you want to be the best person you could be. ... They give you confidence. It's one of the greatest things about them."

During the '90s, when Chris and Sally lived in the Richmond area, she had substantial knee surgery, and the recovery was long and difficult, with periods in which it seemed there was no progress. Pat came to visit. Chris remembers the scene vividly:

Pat had gone out with Sally to help her exercise, and they were on the front sidewalk. Chris watched from inside. Though he could not hear their conversation, he watched as Pat patiently encouraged Sally, supporting her, talking her through this very low point in her life, for what Chris recalls as two hours.

Pat himself loves to walk, Chris said. "It seemed like he could just go on forever, walking." He would go swimming as well, and gave the impression that it was a completely normal thing to swim without hands or forearms.

"He never complains."

Asked to reflect on Pat's politics, Chris said: "He's about the people. He wants opportunity and fairness for everyone. ... He was the ideal judge."

Some years after Sally died, Chris remarried, and he said the Graybeals treat his new wife "as well as you could treat anyone. They put you at ease immediately. They're just that way."

CHAPTER 14

NANCY AND DAD

Nancy Graybeal began her teaching career in 1986, during her father's last term as prosecutor. She knew early on that she wanted to be a teacher. She now teaches eighth-graders near Raleigh, N.C. Like both her parents, she gives off a polite and positive energy, looks younger than she is and, simply by her presence, somehow raises the civilization level of the room. A useful quality for a teacher.

She shares her father's sense of humor.

When she was considering a career, she says, "I thought for a blink" about going into law, probably corporate, but influenced by having watched her mother work she chose teaching. Other parental influences on her included being focused academically, coming to understand the small-town commonality of expectations – of giving back and helping others – and being responsible behind the wheel.

She describes childhood with her sister as a happy time, always with lots of friends and relatives around.

Asked about life at home after the bombing, when occurred when she was 9 and Sally was 11, Nancy said:

"I knew Dad would always have his faith." And it helped greatly to have neighbors and friends rally around, as they did.

"Was I afraid? Not initially … for my sister and me, it was our business to go to school. Children were not involved in adult business. But I just knew he would go back to work, and that seemed right."

"Later," she added, "the neighborhood kids said he was a cool dad. He could flip steaks on the grill with his bare hands."

She paused.

"I never met anyone else like him."

CHAPTER 15

JUDGE

As the prosecutor (commonwealth's attorney) for Montgomery County, I was in a singular job. So it was quite helpful occasionally to be among the few other people in the same sort of position – the members of the Virginia Association of Commonwealth's Attorneys (VACA). We were able to learn from each other and to share best methods and useful insights.

During my quarter-century as a prosecutor, I was honored to serve 14 years on the VACA board of directors and a term as the association's president.

What I learned while in the association made me more effective in Montgomery County, and the combination later helped greatly in the next episode in my life's series of fortunate incidents. In 1989, I became a judge.

As when I became prosecutor, the vacancy was created by the death of the incumbent. And again, I was willing to accept a new opportunity. In fact, I welcomed it. I had been thinking for a few years that serving as a judge would be an appropriate next step in my career. In my last year as prosecutor, I handled 868 cases. It really was time to try to help the community in a different role.

A Circuit Court judge made the formal judicial nomination and, in routine action, it was confirmed by the Virginia General Assembly. I now presided in the Juvenile and Domestic Relations Court, 27th Judicial District – one of the forums where I had worked as prosecutor.

I held this position, concluding with four years as the court's chief judge, until retiring in 1997. In my last year there I handled 5,745 cases.

True to the court's title, many of the people in trouble who appeared before me were juveniles. My main message to them was: You don't need to mess up your life this way.

As often as possible, rather than sentence them to a punishment I sent them to probation officers who could guide them toward solutions and who would check on them periodically. I tried to make it clear that better behavior would be more to their benefit than fighting with their parents or each other. Locking them up was the last choice.

In the domestic relations cases, the majority of disputants did not have lawyers. It was up to me to provide consideration of all aspects. In particular, I would watch the apparent victim carefully and weigh the various potential harms to the family before deciding the case outcome. For example, would jailing one parent severely deprive the rest of the family, financially or otherwise? Or was enforced separation necessary to prevent injury? I had to look at the whole family dynamic to try to decide what the best solution was in each case.

Often, I found, the week or two that came between being arrested and appearing in court gave juveniles as well as adults time and incentive to work out their problems, or at least diminish them enough to keep the peace. Sometimes when defendants appeared before me

I could see that progress was being made, and I would issue a continuance – leaving the case undecided while allowing more time for people to reach their own solutions.

I'd already worked for thirty years in this community either defending or prosecuting those who ran into trouble with the law, and thus had become very familiar with the conditions and people involved in all kinds of ways. For example, I knew many of the teachers and principals who had interacted with juvenile defendants. I knew the officers who made arrests. I knew the capabilities of various government and charitable agencies in dealing with and helping those in trouble. Add to that my childhood of growing up in this area … well, local knowledge was a big help in this job. The more cases that came before me, the more I developed a feel for what the people were doing and trying to do.

When people were brought before me for not paying child support, each situation was different in some way from the others. Each needed to be looked at individually, to ascertain what might work other than jail, which could leave the child with even less support than before.

Custody cases were among the most difficult. Here my aim was for a fair ruling that came the closest to working for all concerned. Sometimes it was easier to address the situation in a private hearing outside the courtroom (a method allowed by the law). Once in a while I decided against making any ruling at all.

In one such instance – a dispute over who should have custody over a teenage boy – as the case unfolded it became very clear to me that one parent viewed the child as a source of income while the boy clearly loved the other parent.

The first parent was contentiously firm against any compromise, and I could see the formal case could go on for a long, non-helpful and expensive time. One day I was sitting in a third-floor room in the court building, holding a private conference with the boy and his uncompromising parent. The discussion was getting nowhere, and finally I turned to the boy and, with a nod toward the exit, said: "That door's not locked."

He stared at me with a look of non-comprehension.

I said again: "That door's not locked."

With a flash of understanding, he bolted. Through the doorway he went and down the stairs. I walked to the window and saw him dash out of the building, toward love and freedom.

Yes, I was not as strict as some judges. There was, for instance, a judge in Martinsville before whom I once appeared as prosecutor in a case that had to be moved from Montgomery County.

This case ended on a real hot day. My side lost, by the way. After the decision, a news reporter spoke up with a request to interview the judge. The judge immediately said no.

Why, the reporter asked.

"You cannot raise a question with me because you're not wearing a jacket in the courtroom," the judge ruled, without regard for the steamy temperature, and stepped down from the bench.

We all walked outside – the attorneys for both sides and the judge, happily removing our jackets – along with the reporter, who then said, "Now can I ask you a question, Judge?"

"No," the judge responded.

"Why not?"

"We're not in the courtroom."

Case closed.

As mentioned, I retired as a district court chief judge in 1997, at age 65. But I wasn't really done, and over the next ten years I enjoyed serving from time to time as a visiting judge in various Virginia counties. Generally I presided over cases that would take at least a week, making the trip from my new home in South Carolina worthwhile. I also continued giving guest lectures for criminal justice classes at Virginia Tech and Radford University. And while in the area, I could also see some longtime friends and check how the landscaping at our old house in Christiansburg was doing.

Ann Carter still lived next door on the backyard side. She recalls:

"I served on several juries during Pat's many years as a prosecutor, and he always showed compassion for both sides." That's not the typical picture people have of prosecutors.

"As my son said later: Pat was always the same, whether he was doing nothing or presiding in court." He was consistently nice, and pleasantly determined.

Sense of humor was always there as well. For example, once when he was invited to attend an event where portraits of all of the court's judges, including his, were to be displayed, "he told me: 'I'm going to the hanging of the judges!'"

CHAPTER 16

A YOUNGER LAWYER'S VIEW

Fred Kellerman is a 1988 graduate of the T.C. Williams School of Law at the University of Richmond, where Pat Graybeal received his law degree 30 years earlier. Kellerman is a defense attorney in Christiansburg. He recollects:

"I was a little boy in Christiansburg, and one day I was with my father in the Thompson-Hagan drugstore near the lunch counter and he motioned toward a man and said, 'That's Pat Graybeal.' I quickly got the realization that Mr. Graybeal was to be respected."

(When told later about this moment, Pat said, "I should have had his dad talk to a lot of people.")

For a while, Fred says, "I rode the school bus with his daughters. Sally was a year older than me." Then Fred's family moved away when he was still a child, and it was not until his wife and he had each graduated from law school that he returned to Christiansburg.

"We set up our law practice there. My very first case as a young lawyer was scheduled before Judge Graybeal. I was so nervous that I threw up the morning of my appearance. But when I actually entered

65

the courtroom everything went wonderfully." Fred saw right away why Pat Graybeal was so respected.

Many of the defendants in Judge Graybeal's courtroom were juveniles, often truants who'd gotten into trouble instead of being in the classroom. Pat would tell them, "If you don't go to your school you can go to mine," which was his way of describing the detention center, Fred recalls.

But what a lot of people didn't know was that Pat made it a regular practice "to have lunch at the detention home with the kids that he put there."

Lawyers who regularly appear in a particular court naturally become judge-watchers. They learn the preferences and non-verbal patterns of each individual on the bench. With Judge Graybeal, Fred soon saw that he preferred that the lawyers' presentations be concise, stick to the relevant facts and get to the point of their side of the case.

If he thought you were going on too long without getting anywhere, "first he would look at you over the top of his glasses, then lift his claws and take his glasses off and set them down."

If you continued to belabor a point already made, "then he'd put his head on his arms."

And if you continued to put forth merely tangential commentary, "he'd rest his arms atop his head, look up and ask, 'Is there anything else?'"

It was all politely done, but Fred learned to take the hint when the glasses first came off.

"About his claws … he was always so natural about having them." Pat never wanted to be thought of as handicapped. Whenever it was appropriate to shake hands, he'd extend his metal one just as if it were flesh, with the implicit anticipation that you would behave normally as well.

One very snowy day when school was canceled, Fred recalled, one of the young assistant prosecutors had an appearance scheduled before Judge Graybeal and had no choice but to take her little boy to court with her. He'd never been to a trial. When Pat entered to take his position, the boy spoke up loudly: "My God, Mom, it's Captain Hook!"

Pat quickly and kindly put everyone (especially the young prosecutor) at ease by coming over and fully explaining to the boy how the metal hooks and prosthetic forearms worked together to accomplish whatever was needed.

Fred recalled: "He seemed to have a positive effect on everyone. Now, there was a long tradition of a collegial bar in this county" – the defense attorneys, the prosecutors and the judges all got along very well and respected the jobs each was there to do. Judges willingly and helpfully trained the newer lawyers. Pat was a leading participant in all that, and appeared to have the respect of everyone – even a certain notoriously crotchety longtime court clerk was devoted to Judge Graybeal.

Kellerman remains an active attorney in the county courts. Asked what he thought was the most difficult aspect for a judge of the Juvenile and Domestic Relations Court, he said:

"The sense of futility when, despite your best efforts, defendants turn out to be a lost cause – and then later seeing their children and then even their grandchildren also in custody and brought before you in court. ... But Judge Graybeal never showed he thought anyone was a lost cause."

He added:

"I have so much respect for Pat as a man, a judge and a friend, and for him and his family considering what they have been through. ... He's a hero."

After Pat Graybeal left the prosecutor's office to become judge in 1989, his successor was assistant commonwealth's attorney Phil Keith. Keith was dealing with his own physical obstacle, having been diagnosed with a brain tumor in 1983. Phil Keith told The Roanoke Times he credited Pat for some of his success:

"He's an amazing man. I really did appreciate the example, how he dealt with the situation. He was a real source of inspiration for me. He never complained, and his sense of humor is unbelievable."

CHAPTER 17

MOVING ON

Jill retired before I did, but she didn't retire much. She became an adjunct instructor at Radford University, training student teachers and teaching classroom management and evaluation of instruction.

Always ready to organize a singing group, she had helped established a community chorus and continued working with church choirs.

During my last days of work as a fulltime judge, a reporter and photographer from The Roanoke Times came by the courthouse to obtain material for a feature about my legal career. During the interview, Lora Puckett, a court clerk, came by with some documents for me to sign.

So, aware of the journalists' needs for a good quote, I asked Lora: "What should I say important about finishing this work?"

"Say you've had a change of heart and you're not going to leave," she responded. That was sweet. But it was time to go.

The retirement gift the family gave ourselves was a cruise around Greece. So here I was afloat again on the ocean, but we didn't have to run dark and silent, offload any tanks or find the right ship for a toothless sailor.

CHAPTER 18

THE RING

Among the losses in the bombing was my wedding ring. That explosion in the driveway caused many immediate concerns, and it was only later that I reflected on where the ring might be. I came to conclude that it was destroyed or lost forever.

After retirement, we moved to South Carolina, to a community where we had bought a vacation condo twenty years earlier. A pleasant house there became our new fulltime home, and Jill created wonderful gardens all around our property.

One day – Dec. 6, 2004 – a small package arrived with a letter. I recognized the return address right away. It was where we had lived in Christiansburg. The house was now owned by Gary and Barbara Long. They had been living there for more than six years, and he was a pastor at the Main Street Baptist Church.

We had revisited the house two years ago and met them. The reason we stopped by then was to take photographs of the rhododendrons in bloom. The property had a profusion of rhododendrons, along with large oaks, all of which we admired greatly. The Longs were very accommodating, and afterward I sent them copies of the photographs, along with a thank-you note on stationery with my initials, JPG.

Anyway, the letter in the package from the Longs explained that Gary had been out raking leaves by the carport and, under a holly shrub, noticed something gold. He picked it up and realized the battered object was a ring. He took it inside to Barbara, and she noticed the inscription on the inside: "JEL to JPG, 7-18-53."

She said she immediately recognized the initials. She had kept the note I'd written to them. And in the package – after 31 years in the dirt and 51 years after it first went onto my hand – was the wedding ring Jill and I had thought was gone forever.

Well, this seemed like a miracle to me. It was pretty emotional. Yet I believe in miracles, and have for a long time. I've had several in my life, and this was another one.

CHAPTER 19

LASTING BONDS

Jill's sister, Katie, and her husband, Dick, regularly traveled with Pat and Jill, particularly in retirement, in the United States, to the Caribbean and a few times to Europe. Katie recalls:

There was always a lot of fun. Dick was quick with the wisecracks and Pat told fine stories and he had all the West Virginia jokes. We really enjoyed being together.

The two men were from very different cultures – Dick a New York City Jew and Pat a Christian from a small Southern town – yet they got along quite well. Dick certainly admired Pat.

Dick would swear a lot and I could see Pat flinch each time, but he never said anything about it. ... Pat's a Southern gentleman, but I think he'd be the same person even if he'd grown up in New York.

Over all the years I've known Pat, there was only one time I saw him lose his temper. It was in a taxi while the four of us were traveling in Spain.

The driver was speeding and swerving recklessly. We suggested he slow down but he kept on. Then Pat broke his cool and just let go.

He demanded that the man immediately drive properly, and if not he must stop the car and let us out.

Pat would visit us in New York and he always got a kick out of the big city ... he loved the crowds, the excitement.

Asked if she had seen Pat change at all over the years, Katie said:

"He's been very consistent – perhaps a little more tolerant and broad-minded later. ... He enlarged his perspective."

She made the point that as a prosecutor for so many years his job was to be the advocate for one side, and that may have carried over a little in people's impressions, while the judge's role can encourage expression of a broader view.

His steady temperament is pretty unusual among all the people I have known, Katie said, especially when he lost a daughter the way he did – "something that just shouldn't happen ... Sally was about as sweet a person as there could be." Pat is not sour, not bitter, not angry, but instead steady and caring, she said.

Katie noted that Pat often says how he is such a lucky man. Considering what he has been through, she said, she once told him:

"What was fortunate was your own personality – that you could overcome all of this."

Throughout, Katie said, Jill has been gallant and steadfast. Her role in supporting and helping him when needed, especially in the months after the attack at their home, came at a large cost, and losing Sally was devastating.

CHAPTER 20

REFLECTIONS

As our children grew, our work lives became more settled and our resources enabled it, we were able to spend more time and money to support education and arts, particularly at Virginia Tech and Radford universities. Two of the results are in Appendix A of this book.

And when we were fully retired, we did what most retirees do. So I won't bore you with the details. I'd just say that it is apparent to us, every day, how fortunate we have been. I guess it's appropriate for music majors that there has been so much harmony in our lives. Jill deserves so much credit for that.

We've been asked about what music has meant to us, and Jill can put it much better than I can.

Jill recalls:

"I always considered music a discipline, and so I was drawn to Bach, Haydn, Handel. Playing their music gave me a sense of accomplishment – totally different from the usual daily work. ... I felt that I had to have music every day," whether listening to it, or playing it, or directing it with the choirs.

Overall, Jill was a working choir director for 27 years, in churches, community groups and schools. In Christiansburg, Pat was a member of the church choir that she directed. Choir practice was not completely smooth, she remembers, because Pat and his brother would sit there telling jokes. But, she adds:

"We met so many wonderful people by being involved with music. And I had high school choirs that could really sing, and the all-county chorus and band. It was a joy to see these young people experiencing the learning of music."

———

Well, this is my story as best as I can remember it. I hope I didn't hurt anybody. All of you who participated have contributed to my education, and for that I am profoundly grateful.

I do not have words sufficiently adequate to thank Jill. It would take a book far larger than this one to properly celebrate how deeply wonderful she is, and all that she has done for me.

I'm one of the luckiest people who ever lived.

PHOTOGRAPHS

PRECEDING PAGE: A fortunate man.
ABOVE: Pat (front center) with his brothers, sister, father and mother, circa 1936.
FACING PAGE: Twenty years old and in officer candidate school in Newport, Rhode Island.

LEFT: Senior year, 1952, at the University of Richmond: Making plans.
BELOW: On July 18, 1953, happiness prevailed.
FACING PAGE: As Jill's sister Katie said: "What an extremely well-suited couple they are."

ABOVE: Daughters Sally, left, and Nancy shared their father's sense of humor.

RIGHT: Nancy says her father has been an inspiration to her.

FACING PAGE: On a cruise around Greece in May 1997, the family celebrates Pat's retirement.

APPENDIX A

SCHOLARSHIPS

The Graybeals and those who have known them have provided for others' futures in ways aimed to help our society. Listed here are two of the ways. The descriptions are provided by Radford University.

The J. Patrick Graybeal Scholarship in Criminal Justice

Family, friends, and colleagues of Judge Graybeal created this scholarship endowment as a lasting tribute in his honor. Judge Graybeal spent four decades in the legal community of the New River Valley. He was first a lawyer, then Montgomery County Prosecutor for 25 years, and finally was a judge for more than seven years. Judge Graybeal is a former member of the RU Foundation's Board of Directors. The scholarship provides aid to a deserving student in Criminal Justice at Radford University.

The scholarship donor is The Honorable J. Patrick Graybeal.

Recipient must be a student majoring in Criminal Justice at Radford University, maintain a minimum GPA of 3.0 and must be a full-time student.

Jill Lobach Graybeal Endowed Scholarship

Mrs. Graybeal established the Jill Lobach Graybeal endowed fund to benefit a student pursuing a degree in Music Education. Mrs. Graybeal graduated from Radford University in 1968 with her M.A. in music. While a member of the Radford University faculty, Mrs. Graybeal served as a field advisor for student teachers. Mrs. Graybeal is a long time supporter of Radford University, especially the Athletic Association, Arts Society and Music Education program.

The scholarship donor is Mrs. Jill Graybeal.

Applicants must be rising juniors or seniors who are pursuing a degree in Music Education and must be full-time students with a minimum 3.0 GPA overall and in the major. Priority consideration is given to students who have demonstrated leadership qualities through participation in extracurricular activities such as music organizations or intercollegiate athletics.

CHRONOLOGY AND OTHER FACTS

Born: March 17, 1932, in Emory, Virginia.

Graduated: from Radford High School and then with a BS in Public School Music from the University of Richmond in Virginia.

Military: Active duty with the U.S. Navy, June 1952-September 1956, including service in Vietnam and Korea, and then in the Naval Reserve, retiring as a lieutenant commander after a total of 21 years of service.

Married: July 18, 1953, in Akron, Ohio. He and Jill later had two daughters, Sally and Nancy. Sally died in 2007.

Law school: Earned a Juris Doctor degree from the T.C. Williams School of Law at the University of Richmond.

Private law practice: In Christiansburg, 1959-64.

Commonwealth's attorney (prosecutor): For Montgomery County, 1964-89.

Judge: 27th Judicial District, Juvenile and Domestic Relations, 1989-97; chief judge 1993-97; visiting judge in Virginia, 1997-2007.

Civic memberships:

- Past president of the Christiansburg-Blacksburg Rotary Club and a Paul Harris Fellow
- St. Paul United Methodist Church of Christiansburg, Virginia, including the church board and 23 years in the choir
- Board of directors, First Virginia Bank of the Southwest
- Radford University Foundation
- Elder, Stephen Minister and Sunday School teacher at First Presbyterian Church, Hilton Head Island, South Carolina
- Board member of the Club Course Property Owners Association.

Professional memberships:

- President of the Virginia Association of Commonwealth's Attorneys (VACA)
- 14 years of service on the Board of Directors for VACA
- Chairman of VACA Services and Training Council
- President of the Montgomery-Floyd-Radford Bar Association
- The American Bar Association
- The 27th Judicial District Bar Association
- The Judicial Liaison Committee
- The District Court System Appeals Panel
- The Executive Committee of the Association of District Court Judges of Virginia
- The Executive Committee of the Juvenile and Domestic Relations Court Judges Association
- Attended conferences of the National Council of Family Court Judges and for judges of Virginia District Courts.

Professional presentations:
- Representing the National College of District Attorneys, presenter on the subject of trial tactics in Philadelphia, New Orleans, Puerto Rico and Camp Lejeune, NC.
- Guest lecturer for classes in criminal justice at Virginia Tech University and Radford University.
- Resource panelist at annual conference for judges of Virginia District Courts.

Civic volunteer activities:
- Fund-raising for the American Cancer Society and local public television
- Attorney for LowCountry Legal Aid
- Volunteer for the Family Circle tennis tournament, the Heritage Classic Foundation's PGA golf tournament, and the Hilton Head International Piano Competition.

Civic presentations:
- Speaker for high school graduations and baccalaureate ceremonies.
- Speaker for meetings of chambers of commerce, Rotary Clubs, Lions Clubs, Kiwanis Clubs, and organizations of firefighters, rescue squads, and other groups.
- Speaker for Radford University awards banquets.
- Inspirational speaker for Handicap Awareness Week in the Radford.

ACKNOWLEDGMENTS

My family – Jill, daughters Sally and Nancy, my brothers and sister, my parents, grandparents and ancestors – all shaped what was positive in my life, as outlined in this book. I am grateful beyond words.

I was blessed with many supportive friends, past and present, more than can be named here. (A few incidents involving them, highly amusing when they happened, will also go unidentified.)

The book's title reflects the good fortune that landed opportunity on me from time to time. Significant examples were delivered by the United States Navy, which provided invaluable schooling, travel experiences and leadership training.

From early childhood through post-graduate seminars, educational institutions enabled me to learn, grow and serve. I particularly appreciate the door opened by Dean William Taylor Muse of the law school at the University of Richmond, who ignored the enrollment deadline and encouraged me into a career that was so ultimately rewarding.

The bombing attack proved how extraordinarily wonderful people can be. I was surrounded with support beyond my knowing – fully heartfelt, effective, caring, curing and inspiring support – beginning almost instantly with the first responders who arrived at that terrible scene and continuing through the community, the legal system and the medical and therapeutic caregivers and specialists. Special thanks to Dr. Ernesto Cube, the ophthalmologist whose skill regarding shrapnel saved my eyesight.

A very significant part of my good luck in the pursuit of justice arrived in those who worked with me – the office staff and my associates in the law. We weren't perfect but we tried (in all senses of the word). In that regard, I certainly owe many thanks to the citizens who kept on re-electing me.

As mentioned way back in Chapter 1, this is my second try at laying out my life in book form. In one more piece of luck, I discovered that telling true stories to a stranger worked out better than going it alone. So I definitely thank my editor and now friend, Alex Cruden.

CPSIA information can be obtained at www.ICGtesting.com
Printed in the USA
LVIW01n1005140817
544913LV00001B/1

* 9 7 8 0 6 9 2 9 2 9 0 2 5 *